CHIRP CHECK

Each night for a week, Debbi and her dad have counted the number of cricket chirps. Debbi knows that if she counts the chirps a single cricket makes in 15 seconds and then adds 37, she should be able to figure out the temperature based on the Fahrenheit scale. Can you fill in Debbi's chart based on the number of chirps each night?

Illustration: Joe Boddy

NIGHT	CHIRPS (in 15 seconds)	TEMPERATURE (degrees Fahrenheit)
Saturday	18	
Sunday	15	
Monday	12	
Tuesday	14	
Wednesday	10	
Thursday	17	
Friday	20	

Answer on page 48

HEAD COUNT

For example, three people are wearing sunglasses. Each person belongs to only one group.

Answer on page 48

Illustration: Rick Geary

1 person: _____	5 people: _____
2 people: _____	6 people: _____
3 people: _sunglasses_	7 people: _____
4 people: _____	8 people: _____

SPORTS REPORT

Match each score with a value from 1 to 10.

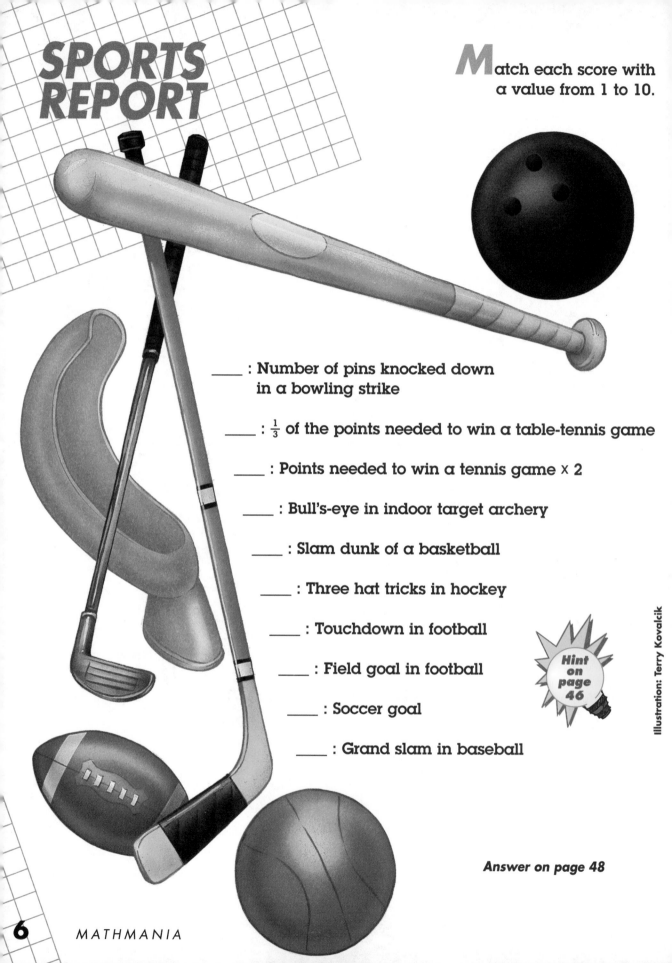

____ : Number of pins knocked down in a bowling strike

____ : $\frac{1}{3}$ of the points needed to win a table-tennis game

____ : Points needed to win a tennis game × 2

____ : Bull's-eye in indoor target archery

____ : Slam dunk of a basketball

____ : Three hat tricks in hockey

____ : Touchdown in football

____ : Field goal in football

____ : Soccer goal

____ : Grand slam in baseball

Hint on page 46

Illustration: Terry Kovalcik

Answer on page 48

WHAT TO PICK?

Tina has 200 tickets. How many different ways can she spend them? She will try to use as many tickets as possible, and she will never choose more than one of the same item. She may have tickets leftover, but never enough to buy another item.

Candy Necklace — 75 — ①

Taffy Candy — 250 — ②

Big Pencil — 200 — ③

Baseball Cap — 100 — ④

Rubber Ball — ⑤ — 70

Bug Key Ring — 175 — ⑥

Whizzer Top — 140 — ⑦

Jelly Beans — ⑧

Smiley Erasers — ⑨ — 60

Stickers — 40 — ⑩

Notebook — 50 — ⑪

Jacks and Ball — 95 — ⑫

125

Answer on page 48

Hint on page 46

Illustration: Doug Cushman

LODGING LOGIC

It's vacation time and a lot of families are on the road.

The Rhodes
Their hotel is between the Dukes' and the Travellis'.

The Karrs
They are sleeping in the hotel next to the Quinns'.

The O'Nighters
Their hotel address is all odd numbers.

The Kings
The address of their hotel can be counted exactly halfway between the highest address and the lowest address.

The Quinns
Their hotel address is three consecutive numbers in order.

The Dukes
Their hotel address is less than the address of the O'Nighters' hotel.

The Princes
They are staying in the last hotel on the right side of the highway.

The Travellis
They are staying in an even-numbered hotel.

Answer on page 48

Hint on page 46

Use the clues to determine the hotel in which each family is spending the night.

9

LUCKY PYRAMID

To recover the lost treasure, start at the bottom and work your way to the top, collecting gold coins. But in order to enter the secret chamber at the top, you must have exactly 50 coins. You can start in any of the bottom stones. As you cross each stone, you must add or subtract the coins mentioned. But beware. You can only cross from one stone to a connecting stone, or else you will slide to the bottom.

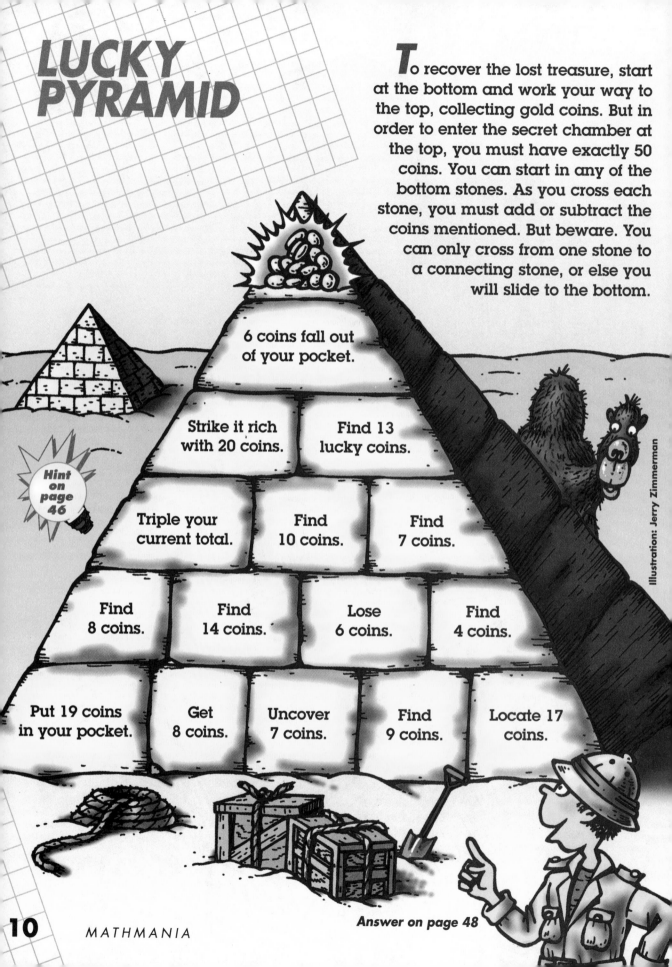

6 coins fall out of your pocket.

Strike it rich with 20 coins.

Find 13 lucky coins.

Triple your current total.

Find 10 coins.

Find 7 coins.

Find 8 coins.

Find 14 coins.

Lose 6 coins.

Find 4 coins.

Put 19 coins in your pocket.

Get 8 coins.

Uncover 7 coins.

Find 9 coins.

Locate 17 coins.

Hint on page 46

Illustration: Jerry Zimmerman

Answer on page 48

DOTS A LOT

Connect these dots by 3s to find a big eater.

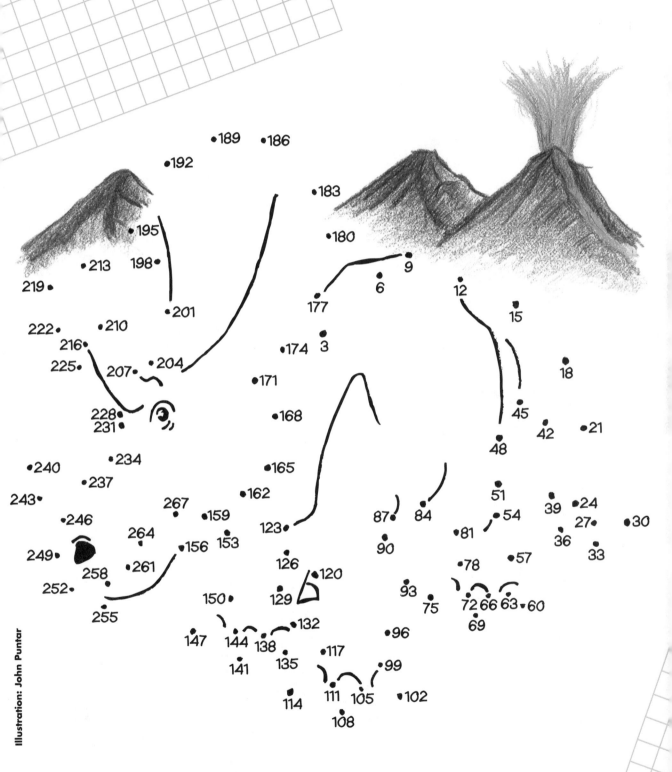

•189 •186

•192

•183

•180

•195

•213 198•

•9
6•

•12
15•

219•

•201

177•

222• •210

216•

225•

207• •204

•174 3

•171

•18

228•
231•

•168

45•
42• •21

48•

•234

•240

•237

•165

51•

243•

•162

39• •24
27• •30

•246

267•

•159

123•

87• 84•

54•

81•

36•
33•

264•

153•

•57

249•

258• •261

•156

126•

•78

252•

150•

129•

120

93•

75•

72 66 63 60

255•

147• 144• 138•

132•

96•

69•

141• 135•

117•

99•

114•

111• 105• 102•

108•

Illustration: John Puntar

SQUARED OFF

Grid 1 (top):

Top row: 3 · · 9 ·
Left column: 6, 7, 8
Right column: 11, 15, 19
Bottom row: 1, 2, · · ·

Grid 2 (bottom):

Top row: 3, 9, ·, ·
Left column: 6, 14, 22
Right column: 13, 11, 10
Bottom row: ·, ·, 21, 28, 35

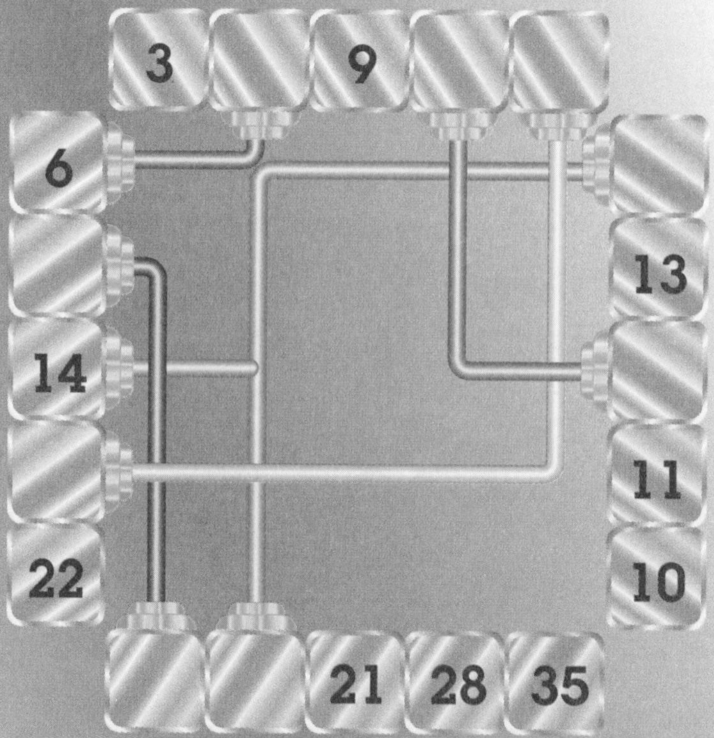

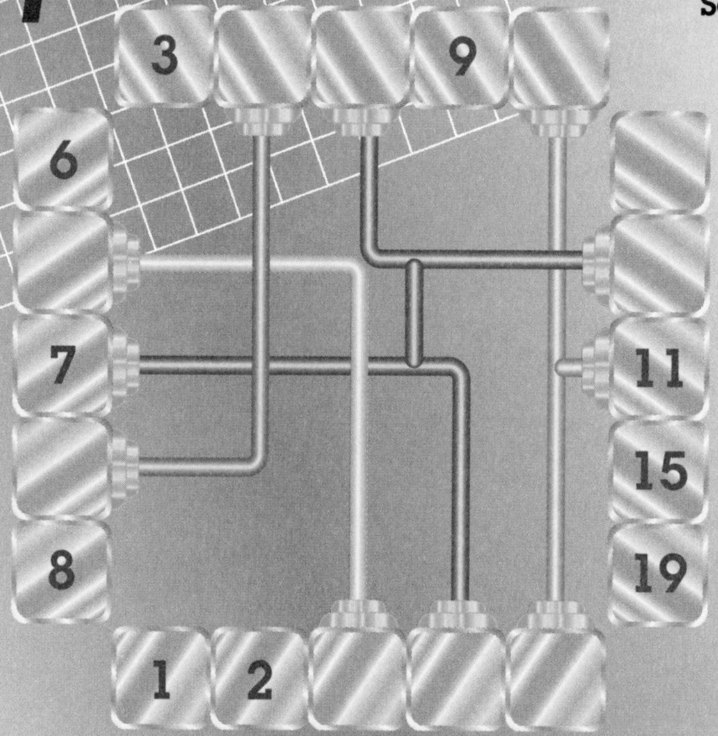

contain the same numbers. Can you follow the patterns to fill in all the squares?

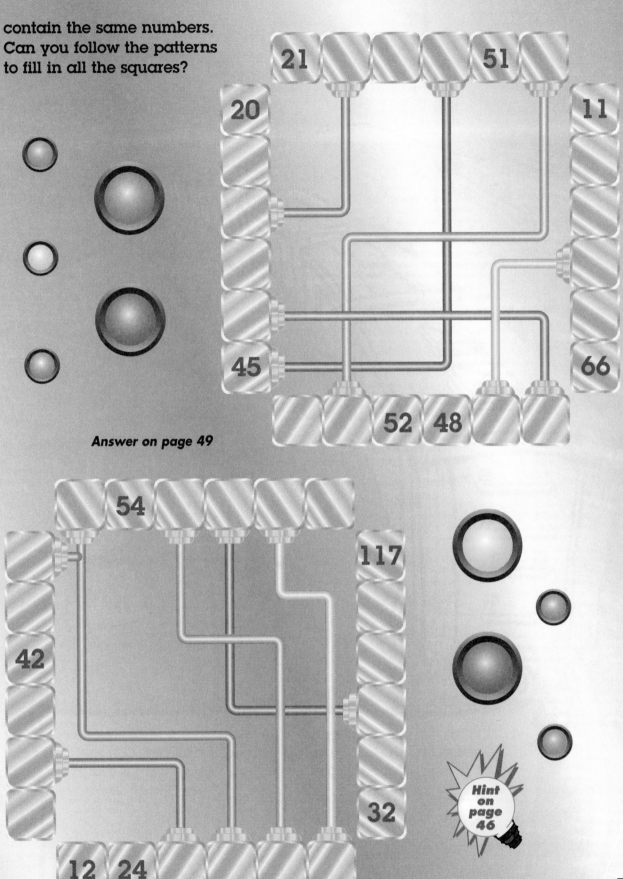

21 51 11 20 45 52 48 66

54 117 42 32 12 24

Answer on page 49

Hint on page 46

TRACKING TROUBLE

You can keep this train on the right track by figuring out the color of each car and the cargo each car is carrying.

Answer on page 49

Illustration: Jim Downer

1. Without including the engine, the order of the train cars is as follows: the car carrying lumber, the second car, the car carrying coal, the black car, and the car carrying pigs.

2. The car carrying automobiles is blue.

3. Car 5 is not brown.

4. The yellow car is not carrying coal, nor is it car 5.

5. The red car is not the one carrying the animal feed.

FAMOUS NAME

Illustration: Kit Wray

If you connect the dots in the order listed, you will find the name of the person described in this autobiography.

I was born in 1897 in Kansas. Even from an early age, I knew that I wanted to fly. I was the first woman to cross the Atlantic Ocean by air as a passenger, and I was also the first woman to fly across it alone. In 1937, while I was trying to fly around the world solo, my airplane disappeared over the Pacific Ocean.

A B C D E F G H I J K L M N O

1 . . . .
2 . . . .
3 . . . .
4 . . . .
5 . . . .
6 . . . .

A1-B1   C1-D2   F1-G1   K1-L1   A4-B4   C4-D4   E4-F4   I4-J4

K4-L4   M4-O4   A2-B2   F2-G2   K2-L2   A5-B5   C5-D5   E5-F5

G5-H5   I5-J5   K5-L5   F3-G3   H3-I3   A6-B6   A1-A3   B1-B3

C1-C3   E1-E3   F1-F3   H1-H3   J1-J3   K1-K3   L1-L3   A4-A6

C4-C6   D4-D6   E4-E6   F4-F5   G4-G6   H4-H6   I4-I6   J4-J6

K4-K6   L4-L5   N4-N6   D2-E1   E5-F6   K5-L6

Answer on page 49

ALL FALL DOWN

The heights of 20 of the world's most spectacular waterfalls are cascading through this grid. First solve the problems to get the heights. Then find the heights in the grid by looking

WATERFALL	ELEVATION	COUNTRY
		Venezuela
Angel	803 × 4 _____	United States
Yosemite	97 × 25 _____	Norway
Mardalsfossen (southern)	1099 + 1050 _____	South Africa
Tugela	1850 + 164 _____	New Zealand
Sutherland	2000 – 96 _____	United States
Ribbon	403 × 4 _____	Guyana
Great	400 × 4 _____	British Columbia
Della	1200 + 243 _____	Brazil
Glass	1500 – 175 _____	Switzerland
Trummelbach	3936 ÷ 3 _____	United States
Silver Strand	830 + 340 _____	Australia
Wallaman	1500 – 363 _____	Australia
Wollomombi	100 × 11 _____	Norway
Skykje	492 × 2 _____	United States
Feather	64 × 10 _____	United States
Snoqualmie	134 × 2 _____	United States
Taughannock	1075 ÷ 5 _____	Canada-United States
Niagara American	91 × 2 _____	Canada-United States
Niagara Horseshoe	200 – 27 _____	United States
Yellowstone (upper)	654 ÷ 6 _____	

across, up, down, backward, or diagonally. Circle each answer as you find it. Some digits may appear in more than one answer, and every digit will be used at least once.

```
4  5  1  2  2  8  1
8  1  1  3  1  6  1
9  1  6  1  2  2  9
4  3  9  0  3  5  0
1  4  1  0  0  7  4
2  4  2  5  1  1  6
2  1  3  1  3  7  1
```

Illustration: Rocky Fuller

Answer on page 49

COUNT OFF

If you count from 1 to 100:

1. How many times do you use the number 9?

2. How many times do you use the number 2?

3. Which single digit— 0, 1, 2, 3, 4, 5, 6, 7, 8, or 9— do you use the most?

4. Which single digit— 0, 1, 2, 3, 4, 5, 6, 7, 8, or 9— do you use the least?

Answer on page 49

Illustration: Jerry Zimmerman

LOPPITS

These are Loppits.

These are not Loppits.

Can you tell which of these are Loppits?

A
B
C
D
E
F
G
H
I
J
K

Hint on page 46

Illustration: David Justice

Answer on page 49

DIGIT DOES IT

That intrepid investiga[tor], Inspector Digit, has a stic[ky] problem. Someone has be[en] putting pieces of bubble gum [all] over the city. The Inspector wa[nts] to grab this sticky sneak bef[ore]

the entire city is stuck together. The only clue is the note stuck here. Can you decipher the code and help the Inspector stop this masticating miscreant?

$\overline{22}\ \overline{5}\ \overline{12}\ \overline{15}$ $\overline{4}\ \overline{3}\ \overline{2}\ \overline{7}\ \overline{5}\ \overline{20}\ \overline{10}\ \overline{11}\ \overline{15}$ $\overline{22}\ \overline{4}\ \overline{13}\ \overline{4}\ \overline{10}$'

$\overline{2}\ \overline{10}\ \overline{4}\ \overline{20}\ \overline{6}$ " $\overline{12}\ \overline{15}\ \overline{11}\ \overline{14}\ \overline{3}\ \overline{22}$ " $\overline{11}\ \overline{15}$ $\overline{4}\ \overline{17}$

$\overline{9}\ \overline{11}\ \overline{14}$ $\overline{20}\ \overline{19}\ \overline{5}\ \overline{1}\ \overline{2}\ \overline{5}$, $\overline{9}\ \overline{11}\ \overline{14}$ $\overline{20}\ \overline{12}\ \overline{3}$

$\overline{7}\ \overline{11}\ \overline{7}$ $\overline{4}\ \overline{3}$ $\overline{10}\ \overline{11}$ $\overline{2}\ \overline{5}\ \overline{5}$ $\overline{21}\ \overline{5}$.

$\overline{10}\ \overline{19}\ \overline{5}$ $\overline{3}\ \overline{14}\ \overline{21}\ \overline{18}\ \overline{5}\ \overline{15}$ $\overline{11}\ \overline{17}$

$\overline{14}\ \overline{3}\ \overline{20}\ \overline{19}\ \overline{5}\ \overline{1}\ \overline{5}\ \overline{22}$ $\overline{2}\ \overline{10}\ \overline{4}\ \overline{20}\ \overline{6}\ \overline{2}$ $\overline{11}\ \overline{17}$

$\overline{13}\ \overline{14}\ \overline{21}$ $\overline{16}\ \overline{5}\ \overline{17}\ \overline{10}$ $\overline{18}\ \overline{5}\ \overline{19}\ \overline{4}\ \overline{3}\ \overline{22}$ $\overline{4}\ \overline{2}$

$\overline{12}\ \overline{16}\ \overline{2}\ \overline{11}$ $\overline{21}\ \overline{9}$ $\overline{19}\ \overline{11}\ \overline{14}\ \overline{2}\ \overline{5}$ $\overline{3}\ \overline{14}\ \overline{21}\ \overline{18}\ \overline{5}\ \overline{15}$

$\overline{11}\ \overline{3}$ $\overline{22}\ \overline{5}\ \overline{3}\ \overline{10}\ \overline{12}\ \overline{16}$ $\overline{22}\ \overline{15}\ \overline{4}\ \overline{8}\ \overline{5}$.

$\overline{20}\ \overline{12}\ \overline{3}$ $\overline{9}\ \overline{11}\ \overline{14}$ $\overline{7}\ \overline{4}\ \overline{5}\ \overline{20}\ \overline{5}$ $\overline{10}\ \overline{19}\ \overline{5}$

$\overline{12}\ \overline{22}\ \overline{22}\ \overline{15}\ \overline{5}\ \overline{2}\ \overline{2}$ $\overline{10}\ \overline{11}\ \overline{13}\ \overline{5}\ \overline{10}\ \overline{19}\ \overline{5}\ \overline{15}$?

$\overline{7}\ \overline{11}\ \overline{7}\ \overline{2}$ $\overline{18}\ \overline{14}\ \overline{18}\ \overline{18}\ \overline{16}\ \overline{5}\ \overline{2}$

Hint on page 46

Answer on page 50

SCRAMBLED PICTURE

Copy these mixed-up wedges onto the next page to unscramble the picture. The letters and numbers

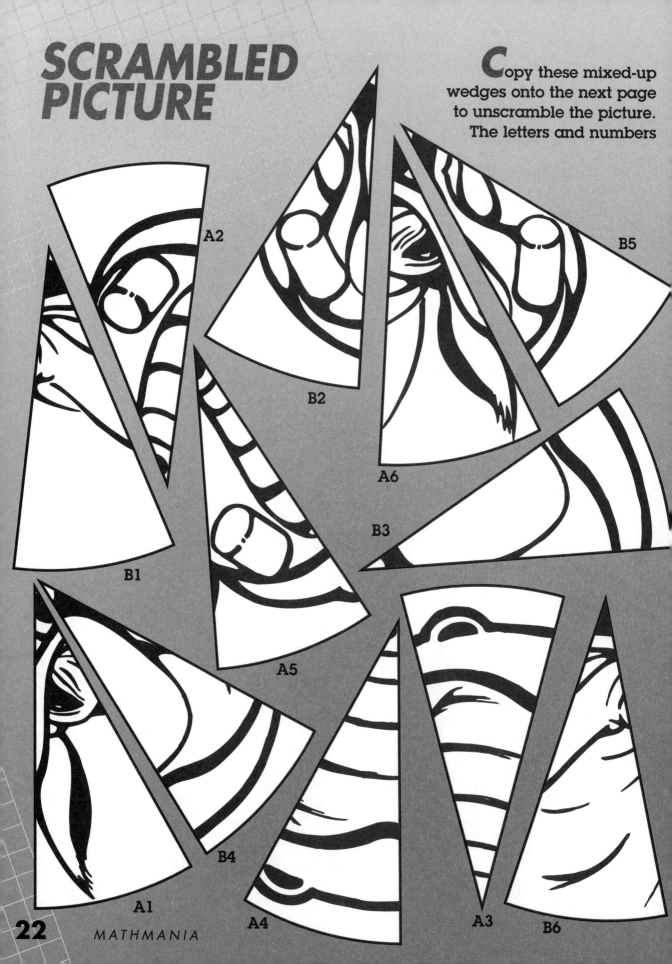

A2

B5

B2

A6

B3

B1

A5

B4

A1

A4

A3

B6

tell you where each wedge
belongs. We've done the
first one, A3, to start you off.

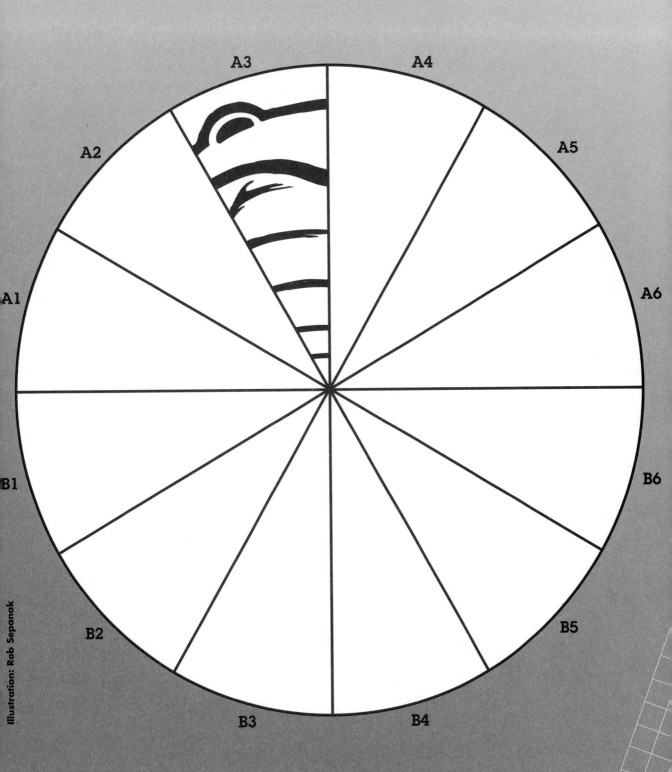

Answer on page 50

SIGN IN

The set of 5s in each problem always equals a different number. Just add the right signs (either +, −, ×, or ÷), then perform the functions to equal the answer shown. Be sure to do the part of the problem that is in parentheses first.

Example: (5 __ 5) __ 5 = 5

(5 ÷ 5) × 5 = 5

1. (5 __ 5) __ 5 = 20

2. 5 __ (5 __ 5) = 4

3. 5 __ 5 __ 5 = 15

4. (5 __ 5) __ 5 = 6

5. (5 __ 5) __ 5 = 2

6. 5 __ (5 __ 5) = 30

7. (5 __ 5) __ 5 = 50

8. 5 __ 5 __ 5 = 125

Illustration: Jerry Zimmerman

Hint on page 46

Answer on page 50

CLOSE CALL

Eight racers came in so fast and so close that the judges couldn't tell who won. The competitors listened to the announcer as he excitedly called out the results. They were able to figure out the order in which everyone finished. Can you figure it out, too?

Illustration: Rick Geary

"Four is before five and after two and three, who are behind six and eight. Seven is last. One is not first, but is before three and after two."

Answer on page 50

CIRCLE SETS

1 red pink

2 family children

3 yellow blue

4 soil mud

5 smog fog

6 jacket pants

7 snow blizzard

26

combine to create the item in the middle. For example, when you combine corn and lima beans, you get succotash. Can you supply the missing item in each set of circles?

corn | **succotash** | **lima beans**

8 — $1.00 | $.25

9 — hydrogen | oxygen

12 — players | team

11 — brunch | lunch

10 — ice cream | milk shake

13 — water | flour

14 — soap | bubbles

15 — copper | tin

Illustration: R. Michael Palan

Answer on page 50

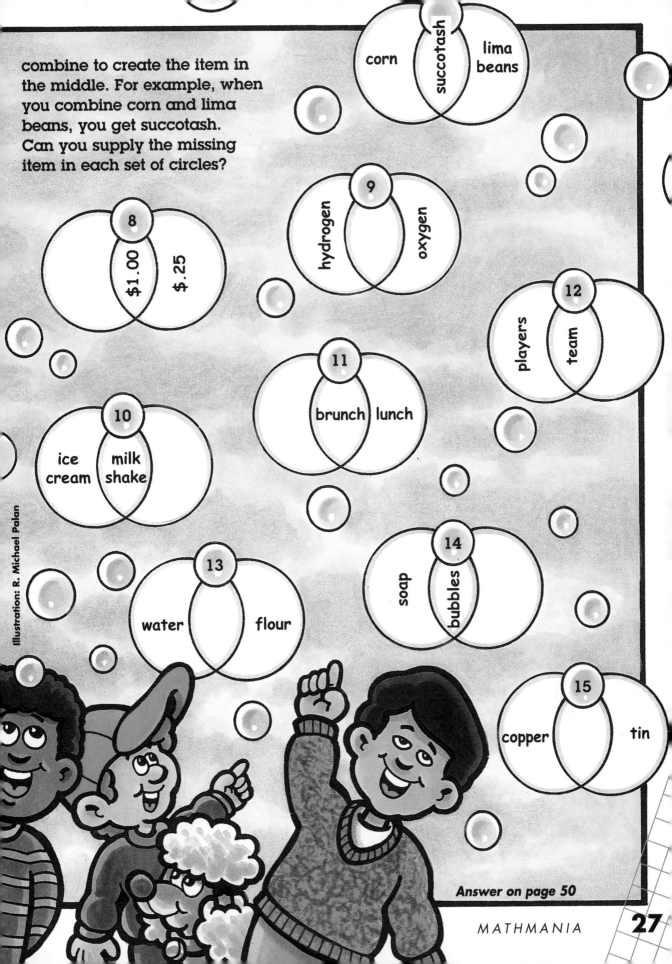

SIMONE SAYS

Simone has a 4-inch square piece of paper. She wants to make a square that is only about $\frac{3}{4}$ the size of the original square. How can she do it without cutting the paper?

Hint on page 47

Answer on page 50

Illustration: R. Michael Palan

TAKE ONE

In each group below, three of the four numbers can be combined to equal 1. Circle the one number that doesn't belong. Once you've done all six, look at the numbers you've circled. You should be able to combine the circled numbers to form two more groups, each of which will equal 1.

Hint on page 47

1. $\frac{1}{4}$ $\frac{1}{2}$ $\frac{1}{5}$ $\frac{2}{8}$

2. 25%   60%   35%   15%

3. 0.5   0.4   0.3   0.2

4. .32   .40   .28   .36

5. 40%   .15 $\frac{3}{4}$ 10%

6. $\frac{1}{4}$ 50%   .25   .29

Answer on page 50

Illustration: David Helton

TWIST AND SHOUT

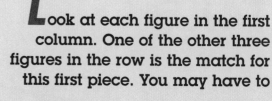

A   **B**   **C**

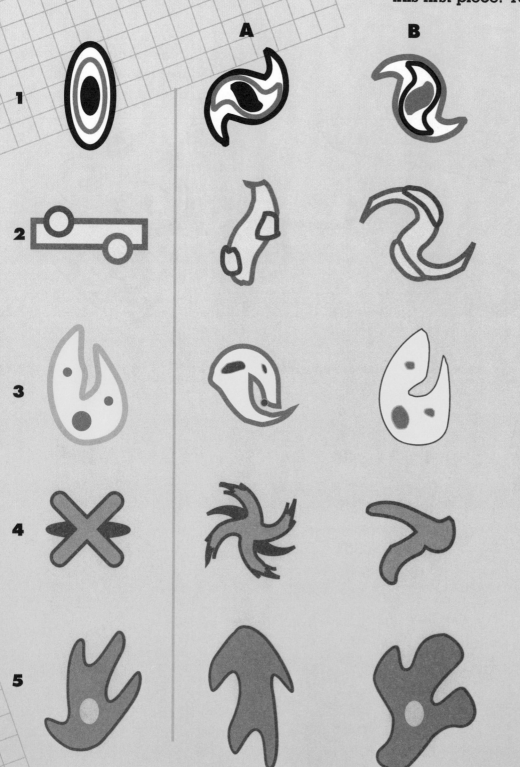

1

2

3

4

5

imagine the piece moving,
twisting, shrinking, or stretching.
But each piece will be the same,
with no added holes or lines.

Hint
on
page
47

A   **B**   **C**

6 G

7 8

8

9

10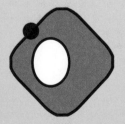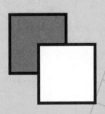

LIBRARY LAUGHS

Dewey has some funny books in his library. To check one out, solve each problem. Then go to the shelves to find the volume with the number that matches each answer. Put the matching letter in the blank beside each answer. Read down the letters you've filled in to find the title and author of the book Dewey just finished reading.

Illustration: Scott Peck

Answer on page 50

$4 \times 2 =$ _____

$8 + 1 =$ _____

$24 - 5 =$ _____

$40 \div 2 =$ _____

$19 - 4 =$ _____

$11 + 7 =$ _____

$27 \div 3 =$ _____

$14 - 11 =$ _____

$3 \div 3 =$ _____

$3 \times 4 =$ _____

$9 - 5 =$ _____

$21 - 20 =$ _____

$5 \times 4 =$ _____

$30 \div 6 =$ _____

$14 + 5 =$ _____

$8 - 6 =$ _____

$5 \times 5 =$ _____

$27 \div 9 =$ _____

$1 \times 1 =$ _____

$10 + 2 =$ _____

$20 - 6 =$ _____

$9 - 5 =$ _____

$25 \div 5 =$ _____

$13 + 5 =$ _____

$9 \times 2 =$ _____

SAND ART

Can you re-create this image without crossing over any lines or removing your pencil from the page?

Illustration: Barbara Gray

Answer on page 51

33

ROOM TO GROW

THE HOME AND REAL ESTATE TABLOID

1. Oversized ranch, 6 bedrooms, 4 baths, large country kitchen, dining room, which leads to enclosed sunroom. Large living room with fireplace. Full usable basement and attic. Nice neighborhood.

2. Large Victorian-style home with 4 bedrooms, each with own bath. Big kitchen-dining room combination, plus a pantry. Elegantly decorated parlor and small library. Living room can accommodate large family. Full attic has been transformed into separate guest room with private bath. Great area for pets. On 2 acres.

Hint on page 47

Illustration: Jim Downer

Read the listings on these pages to find the house that has the most rooms.

A HOME BUYING AND SELLING GUIDE

3. Gracious older farmhouse with 5 bedrooms, 2 baths, large kitchen and dining room, living room, den, mud room, and attached workshop. Quiet area next to wooded state property with stream.

4. Newly built contemporary home with 3 bedrooms, 3 baths, large kitchen-living room combination. Fully furnished office, studio, and small sauna-hot tub room. Library has skylights. Basement is a large recreation room. Outside property features a pond and large field.

Answer on page 51

MATHMAGIC

Here's a quick trick.

Get a square piece of paper and give it to a friend.

Tell your friend that if he can tear the paper into four equal pieces, you'll give him a quarter.

Very impressive.

And here's your quarter.

Illustration: Marc Nadel

COLOR BY NUMBERS

Illustration: Rob Sepanak

Use the key to color the spaces and you'll find a place for some deep conversation.

Answer on page 51

KEY

1 dot—Black
2 dots—White
3 dots—Blue
4 dots—Green

5 dots—Yellow
6 dots—Orange
7 dots—Red

FOLDING FUN

Each piece of paper here can be folded to make one of the objects on the shelves.

Can you match each finished object with its flat diagram?

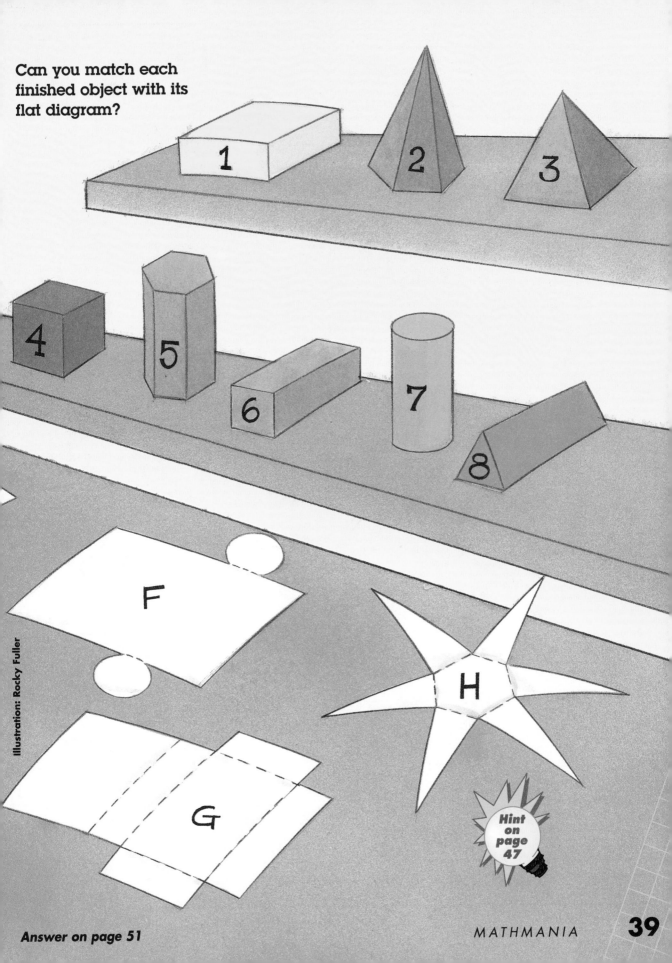

Illustration: Rocky Fuller

Hint on page 47

Answer on page 51

SUM RIDDLE

To find our riddle and its answer, you'll need to solve some problems. When you find the answers, put the letter of each problem in the space above the number that matches the answer.

A	B	C	E	F
637	152	627	490	307
+245	+439	+368	+268	+892

H	I	L	M	N	O
939	785	625	413	652	658
+384	+362	+785	+589	+73	+92

R	S	T	W
1,567	2,027	21,234	322
+9,687	+8,596	+36,897	417
			+68

Illustration: Marc Nadel

―――――――――――――――――――――――――――――――――――――
807 1,323 882 58,131   1,410 758 58,131 58,131 758 11,254

―――――――――――――――――――――――――――――――――――――
995 750 1,002 758 10,623   882 1,199 58,131 758 11,254   882 ?

―――――――――――――――――――――――――――――――――――――
882 1,410 1,410   750 1,199   58,131 1,323 758 1,002

CHALK

SHELF SERVE

Four different types of cars are in this display. The cars of the same color cost the same amount, either $2, $4, $6, or $7. The totals for each row across, as well as for each column down, are given on the tags. Can you help figure out the individual prices of the cars in each color group?

Illustration: David Helton

$22.00

$15.00

$20.00

$17.00

$18.00

$17.00

$19.00

$20.00

Hint on page 47

Answer on page 51

MEDIEVAL MEASURES

Come with us now to those thrilling days of centuries past and see how you would measure up to these knights of old.

1. When a knight said he would return in a fortnight, he came back 14 days later. His squire might return in a sennight, which was half a fortnight. How many days was a sennight?

D. 10 days
E. 8 days
K. 7 days

2. If a baker needed a firlot's worth of grain, she would get a quarter of a boll's worth. A boll equals 6 bushels. If there are 8 gallons in just 1 bushel, how many gallons are in a firlot?

A. 6   I. 12   U. 24

Answer on page 51

Illustration: Michael Austin

If you circle the letters of the right answers, you should be able to spell out the best job in town.

3. If the king's workers were digging a moat around the castle, they would measure things in ells, fathoms, or cables. An ell equals 4 feet, while a fathom on land equals $5\frac{1}{2}$ yards. If a cable equals 120 fathoms, how many ells are in a cable?

K. 475   N. 495   R. 500

4. A cubit equals 2 spans, while 1 span equals 2 hands plus an additional inch. This 2 hands and an inch is equal to 3 palms. One hand is 4 inches in length. How big is a cubit? How big is a palm?

E. cubit = 3 inches; palm = 18 inches
G. cubit = 18 inches; palm = 3 inches
L. cubit = 13 inches; palm = 8 inches

Hint on page 47

43

BLOCK OF 20

Fill in the blanks of this grid so that the numbers in each block of four squares total 20. Only single digits are used, and some digits may be repeated within the same block.

For example:

8	3	4
2	7	6
6	5	2

Hint
on
page
47

	6		0	
3		2		5
	7	8		
4				
	9			

POCKET CHANGE

Hint on page 47

Jesse, Jason, Jon, and Jerome each put five coins into one pile. They wrote down how much each person put in, and now they're trying to give the money back. Can you tell how much money they had altogether? And can you give the appropriate coins back to the right people so that all the coins are gone?

Illustration: Bill Colrus

JESSE.....30¢
JASON.....77¢
JON.....77¢
JEROME...78¢
.....25¢

Answer on page 51

HINTS AND BRIGHT IDEAS

*T*hese hints may help with some of the trickier puzzles.

COVER
Think of the lowest number that can be evenly divided by all the numbers given.

SPORTS REPORT (page 6)
An archery bull's-eye is worth half the number of pins knocked down in a bowling strike. You need 21 points to win at table tennis.

WHAT TO PICK? (page 7)
Tina might choose a candy necklace (75), a rubber ball (70), and some stickers (40). That totals 185. She doesn't have enough left for another pick. What other combinations could she make?

LODGING LOGIC (pages 8-9)
Start with the Princes. Then look for the Quinns' hotel. Zero is considered an even number.

LUCKY PYRAMID (page 10)
Start in the bottom row with the block that gives you 7 coins. Then move up to a space that will give you a total of 21 coins.

SQUARED OFF (pages 12-13)
Look for different sequences on each side.

LOPPITS (page 19)
All Loppits have straight sides and four hairs on the long tail. What two other things do Loppits have in common?

DIGIT DOES IT (pages 20-21)
The word *Inspector* appears in the note's greeting.

SIGN IN (page 24)
When you need one part of your equation to equal 1, always go with the ÷ sign.

SIMONE SAYS (page 28)
Though Simone can't cut the paper, she can fold it. It may help if you had a square piece of paper of your own to work with. $\frac{3}{4}$ of 4 inches would be 3 inches. Simone's new figure is very close.

TAKE ONE (page 29)
The trick in each group is to make the pieces add up to 1. In question 3, 0.4 = $\frac{4}{10}$ or $\frac{2}{5}$; 0.5 and 0.3 equal 0.8. If you add 0.2, you get 1.0 or 1. Different fractions can stand for the same amount. For example, 0.5, $\frac{1}{2}$, and 50% are all ways to measure half of something. 40% = $\frac{2}{5}$.

TWIST AND SHOUT (pages 30-31)
Try to imagine each object from a different view. What might it look like stretched out or from the back?

ROOM TO GROW (pages 34-35)
Include the bath as one room.

FOLDING FUN (pages 38-39)
You have to use your imagination to figure out what these objects look like. When you see a circle on the flat diagram, look for a completed shape with a circular side. All the fold lines are given.

SHELF SERVE (page 41)
Start at the row with three yellow cars. If these three cars have the same value, how much is the last car worth in order for the row to have a value of 20?

MEDIEVAL MEASURES (pages 42-43)
Don't let the unusual names throw you off the track. Concentrate on the numbers. Writing the problems out may help. For example, 1 fortnight = 14 days. One sennight is $\frac{1}{2}$ of 14.

BLOCK OF 20 (page 44)
A block is formed by any four adjacent squares that make up a new square. Check the example.

POCKET CHANGE (page 45)
Start with Jerome. Which five coins equal $.25?

ANSWERS

COVER
30

CHIRP CHECK (page 3)

NIGHT	TEMPERATURE
Saturday	55°
Sunday	52°
Monday	49°
Tuesday	51°
Wednesday	47°
Thursday	54°
Friday	57°

HEAD COUNT (pages 4-5)
We counted these groups.
You may have found others.
1 person: straw hat
2 people: bald
3 people: sunglasses
4 people: scarves or neckties
5 people: bow ties
6 people: eyeglasses
7 people: eating ice cream
8 people: baseball caps

SPORTS REPORT (page 6)
10: Number of pins knocked down in
    a bowling strike
7: $\frac{1}{3}$ of the points needed to win a table-
    tennis game
8: Points needed to win a tennis game × 2
5: Bull's-eye in indoor target archery
2: Slam dunk of a basketball
9: Three hat tricks in hockey
6: Touchdown in football
3: Field goal in football
1: Soccer goal
4: Grand slam in baseball

WHAT TO PICK? (page 7)
Tina has 28 different choices:

3	5, 12	1, 5, 10	8, 9, 10
6	5, 11	5, 9, 10	4, 8, 10
7, 9	7, 8	1, 9, 10	8, 10, 12
1, 4	10, 11	1, 8, 9	9, 10, 12
7, 10	9, 11	5, 8, 9	
4, 5	1, 11	1, 5, 8	
4, 12	8, 11	1, 8, 10	
1, 12	4, 9, 10	5, 8, 10	

LODGING LOGIC (pages 8-9)
532: Dukes   789: Quinns
533: O'Nighters   800: Travellis
548: Rhodes   865: Karrs
703: Kings   874: Princes

LUCKY PYRAMID (page 10)

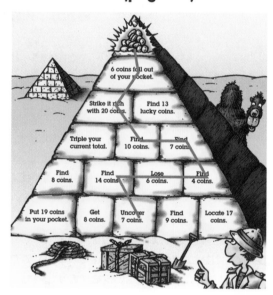

DOTS A LOT (page 11)

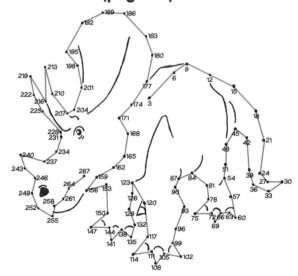

SQUARED OFF (pages 12-13)

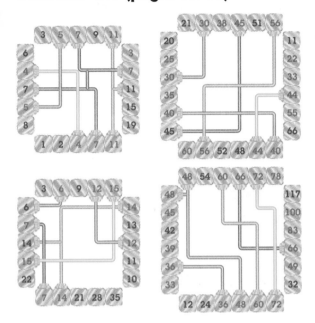

ALL FALL DOWN (pages 16-17)

WATERFALL	ELEVATION
Angel	$803 \times 4 = 3212$
Yosemite	$97 \times 25 = 2425$
Mardalsfossen	$1099 + 1050 = 2149$
Tugela	$1850 + 164 = 2014$
Sutherland	$2000 - 96 = 1904$
Ribbon	$403 \times 4 = 1612$
Great	$400 \times 4 = 1600$
Della	$1200 + 243 = 1443$
Glass	$1500 - 175 = 1325$
Trummelbach	$3936 \div 3 = 1312$
Silver Strand	$830 + 340 = 1170$
Wallaman	$1500 - 363 = 1137$
Wollomombi	$100 \times 11 = 1100$
Skykje	$492 \times 2 = 984$
Feather	$64 \times 10 = 640$
Snoqualmie	$134 \times 2 = 268$
Taughannock	$1075 \div 5 = 215$
Niagara American	$91 \times 2 = 182$
Niagara Horseshoe	$200 - 27 = 173$
Yellowstone	$654 \div 6 = 109$

TRACKING TROUBLE (page 14)

CAR COLOR	CARGO
1—Yellow	Lumber
2—Blue	Automobiles
3—Brown	Coal
4—Black	Animal Feed
5—Red	Pigs

The five cargo items are lumber, coal, pigs, automobiles, and animal feed. The five colors are black, blue, brown, yellow, and red. Clue 2 says the car with the automobiles is blue. Clue 1 suggests that this can only be car 2. Clue 4 says the yellow car isn't carrying coal, nor is it car 5. So the yellow car can only be car 1. If car 5 is not brown, then car 3 must be brown. That leaves car 5 as the red car. But that car doesn't have animal feed, which can only go in car 4.

COUNT OFF (page 18)

1. The number 9 is used 20 times (9, 19, 29, 39, 49, 59, 69, 79, 89-99).
2. The number 2 is used 20 times, too (2, 12, 20, 21, 22-29, 32, 42, 52, 62, 72, 82, 92).
3. The number 1 is the digit that gets used the most—21 times (1, 10, 11-19, 21, 31, 41, 51, 61, 71, 81, 91, 100).
4. 0 is the digit that gets used the least—11 times (10, 20, 30, 40, 50, 60, 70, 80, 90, 100).

FAMOUS NAME (page 15)

LOPPITS (page 19)

D, J, K

DIGIT DOES IT (pages 20-21)

Dear Inspector Digit,
Stick around. Or if you "chewse," you can pop in to see me. The number of unchewed sticks of gum left behind is also my house number on Dental Drive. Can you piece the address together?
Pops Bubbles

α-12	f-17	l-16	r-15	w-1
b-18	g-13	m-21	s-2	y-9
c-20	h-19	n-3	t-10	
d-22	i-4	o-11	u-14	
e-5	k-6	p-7	v-8	

We found 30 sticks.
How many did you find?

SCRAMBLED PICTURE (pages 22-23)

SIGN IN (page 24)

1. (5 × 5) − 5 = 20
2. 5 − (5 ÷ 5) = 4
3. 5 + 5 + 5 = 15
4. (5 ÷ 5) + 5 = 6
5. (5 + 5) ÷ 5 = 2
6. 5 + (5 × 5) = 30
7. (5 + 5) × 5 = 50
8. 5 × 5 × 5 = 125

CLOSE CALL (page 25)

The racers finished in this order (from first to last): 6, 8, 2, 1, 3, 4, 5, 7.

CIRCLE SETS (pages 26-27)

1. white
2. parents
3. green
4. water
5. smoke
6. suit
7. wind
8. $.75
9. water
10. milk
11. breakfast
12. coach
13. paste
14. water
15. bronze

SIMONE SAYS (page 28)

Simone can fold the paper in this way.

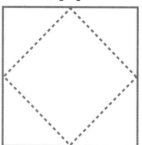

TAKE ONE (page 29)

1. $\frac{1}{4}$ $\frac{1}{2}$ $\frac{2}{8}$

2. 25%   60%   15%

3. 0.5   0.3   0.2

4. .32   .40   .28

5. .15 $\frac{3}{4}$ 10%

6. $\frac{1}{4}$ 50%   .25

Leftover numbers: $\frac{1}{5}$, 35%, 0.4, .36, 40%, .29. These can be formed into two groups that both equal 1:
$\frac{1}{5}$, 0.4, 40% and 35%, .36, .29.

TWIST AND SHOUT (pages 30-31)

1—A	6—A
2—B	7—C
3—C	8—B
4—A	9—B
5—B	10—B

LIBRARY LAUGHS (page 32)

4 × 2 = 8	H	8 − 6 = 2	B
8 + 1 = 9	I	5 × 5 = 25	Y
24 − 5 = 19	S	27 ÷ 9 = 3	C
40 ÷ 2 = 20	T	1 × 1 = 1	A
19 − 4 = 15	O	10 + 2 = 12	L
11 + 7 = 18	R	20 − 6 = 14	N.
27 ÷ 3 = 9	I	9 − 5 = 4	D
14 − 11 = 3	C	25 ÷ 5 = 5	E
3 ÷ 3 = 1	A	13 + 5 = 18	R
3 × 4 = 12	L	9 × 2 = 18	R
9 − 5 = 4	D		
21 − 20 = 1	A		
5 × 4 = 20	T	**HISTORICAL DATES**	
30 ÷ 6 = 5	E	by Cal N. Derr	
14 + 5 = 19	S		